A Lifetime in Steam

John Procter

ISBN 978-1-907094-69-9

FOREWORD

For a great many of us of the older generation, the fascination with steam locomotives, is something we grew up with in our youth, and once drawn in it seemed to get into the blood and has certainly in my case as with many, lasted a lifetime.

So it was with John Procter, who along with many others of our generation went about collecting engine numbers to start with, and went on organised railway installation visits run by such organisations as the Railway Travel & Correspondence Society (RCTS)

John developed his interest further by recording the railway scene in film, both still photography, and on cine film.

It is good to note that at the time of writing, it is still possible for us to witness steam locomotives at work almost every week somewhere or other in the British Isles on the National Network, something I'm sure we would not have believed possible back in the 1960's when steam traction became redundant on British Railways.

Today's steam operations are excellently organised and run by dedicated groups of people both in the private sector, largely locomotive owning groups, and current railway operating companies TOC's.

But one thing they can never recapture is the Infrastructure and the atmosphere of the old steam railway. Long gone are the marshalling yards, the coaching stock sidings, the great engine sheds full of smoke and grime, oil and water mixed with the smell of steam coal. The great stations with their overall roofs such as Nottingham Victoria, Glasgow St Enoch and others truly Cathedrals of Steam, not like the bus shelters of today.

In our day the railway was lambasted by the press and the public alike for the lack of cleanliness, and the staleness of the meat pie, our engines weren't always clean and polished, like the museum pieces of today, they were work stained and alive, and toiled throughout the day and night to get the nation to work and bring the goods to Town and City. The men that worked the railway were made of sterner stuff than many are today, and put up with some terrible working conditions, but who among them do you hear complaining, the majority recall their toil with a feeling of pride and honour, and a love of their old charges.

The photographs in this book are representative of the railway we remember, showing the old order, the transition of the railway after the last World War through to the end of steam, which so coincided with the development of road haulage and a general demise of our beloved railway.

Be you a fan of the Western, Southern, Midland or Eastern Region of British Railways, there is something here for all.

There will be many of you that will say to yourselves, "I remember that" and you will be filled with that warm glow of nostalgia.......enjoy.

David Richards, December 2010

First published in the United Kingdom by Book Law Publications 2011

382 Carlton Hill, Nottingham NG4 1JA

Printed and bound by The Amadeus Press, Cleckheaton, West Yorkshire

John Procter
Photographer
27.02.1934 to 25.03.2007

John Procter was born and raised in Nottingham during the 1930's and spent a lot of his younger years watching his beloved steam locomotives at work on the Great Central Railway.

After the end of hostilities at the age of Fifteen John started work and with some money in his pocket was able to purchase his first still camera. His early pictures like most of his contemporaries were not as good as he would have liked, but not being one to be put off John honed his photographic skills in the ensuing years.

The earliest pictures I have of John's are recorded as being taken in early 1952 and feature a Midland 3F on a freight working, and from that day forward his pictures just got better and better.

A succession of cameras and becoming a member of the East Midlands RCTS helped in progressing his photographic prowess throughout the 1950s and on into the Sixties as John travelled extensively across the British Isles up to the end of steam on Britain's railways and even in Germany after that, such was his love of steam.

In the early part of the 1963 John took up the mantle of cine cameraman, recording the last years of his beloved Great Central Railway in detail, the evidence of which is available on DVD from this Publisher to this day.

I was to meet John as a near neighbour upon moving into the Newthorpe area of Nottingham in 1981 and with both of us keen railway modellers and railway enthusiasts, soon struck up a great friendship which, although I later moved away to work, lasted until John's death in 2007.

During those twenty six years I was to introduce John to the John Player Railway society in Nottingham and got him to show his wonderful cine films to the membership there, where they were so well received, and held in such high regard, that eventually led to getting his material digitally re-mastered and put onto DVD.

Upon his death at the age off seventy three John left his entire collection to me, and ever since then it has been my intention to have some of his photographic work published, as a tribute to his friendship not only to me, but all those that knew him.

Rarely does work of this magnitude come to the surface these days, but thanks to the good offices of Dave Allen of BOOK LAW publishing, this will now be redressed.

Please now enjoy and relive the great days of Britain's post war railways under steam.

All remuneration received by the author in connection with this publication will be donated to Cancer research in John's name.

David Richards December 2010

3

David Richards

Compiler & Author

Better known as a video cameraman Dave Richards has been part of the PSOV team working alongside Karl Jauncey who produces some of the finest and best known contemporary steam videos of the past twenty three years, with two volumes a year covering the exploits of Britain's preserved steam locomotives on the National Railway system.

David has been an avid steam locomotive enthusiast ever since his father took him along to his grandfathers allotment to help pick the fruit and vegetables, adjacent to the Great Central Railway at Birstall in Leicestershire.

His earliest recollections are of Leicester based A3 Pacific's *Galtee More*, and *Sir Frederick Banbury*, plying their trade on the Marylebone Manchester services of the 1950s.

During a career lasting thirty six years in the insurance industry David moved about the Midlands in connection with his work, which in 1981 brought him to Newthorpe in Nottinghamshire where his near neighbour was John Procter, who became a lifelong friend.

Many hours would be spent looking through John's collection of B/W negatives and box after box of colour slides, which he had taken over a great many years. He had travelled extensively both on his own and with The Railway Correspondence & Travel Society (RCTS) where he had been an active member for many years.

Here then, in a tribute to John's photographic prowess and friendship, is just a sample of his B/W collection taken from the four corners of the British Railway system spanning the years from 1952 through to the end of steam in Britain in 1968.

I'm sure it will evoke many memories for all steam lovers throughout the UK.

Front Cover Picture: A4 Pacific No.60004 Sir William Whitelaw, of Edinburgh Haymarket depot runs into Inverkeithing station from the North with an Aberdeen to Edinburgh express on 27th May 1958.

Back Cover Picture: British Railways Standard Pacific 72000 Clan Buchanan heads North past Scout Green on the accent of Shap, with a very lightweight train.

Title Page Picture: British Railways Class 9F 92069 ready to depart with the South Yorkshireman Express from Nottingham Victoria Station to London Marylebone 19th July 1958.

The Earl & Countess

Narrow Gauge Sisters

Oswestry Works

Churchward Shunting Engine

Right Hand Drive

Swindon Running Shed

Dean Rebuild from 1897

Birkenhead Survivor

Birkenhead 19th April 1953

75020 pilots Ex GWR 22xx

Cambrian Holiday Special

Between Wrexham & Chester

Prototype Castle 4073 Caerphilly Castle

Great Western Pride

Awaiting restoration at Swindon

4136 pilots a Hall Class 4.6.0

A Helping Hand

Severn Tunnel Junction

Milk Tankers

Two Panniers for Three Cocks

Three Cocks Junction

Departing Pontypool Road For Newport

Newport Bound

4948 Northwick Hall 19th July 1959

5645 Collett Tank

South Wales Collier

Gas Works Pontypool Road

6003 King George 1V

Paddington Departure

5th May 1961 Photo by Author

6009 King Charles 11 Leamington Spa

26th September 1959 Photo by Author

Cambrian Coast Express

6384 at Hawkridge Jnc.

Churchward Mogul

Westbury bound

6735 & Friends

A Pannier...How many would you Like?

Newport Gwent

6869 Resolven Grange

Par Excellence

Departs for Lostwithiel

6968 Woodcock Hall

Bristol Bound

Departs Westbury

Standard 4 pilots 7818 Granville Manor   Moat Lane heading West

Cambrian Super Power

Pannier 8795

Wet Day Working

St. Phillips Marsh 3rd April 1960

Dukedog 9014

Croes Newydd

Ready for Coaling

Fowey Auto Train

Lostwithiel Cornwall

Cambourne for Five & a Tanner

Short Framed M7 30241

Nine Elms Pilot

Nine Elms Shed Yard

30453 King Arthur

Water for The King

Nine Elms Yard

S15 30477

Standard Five 73089

Nine Elms Variety

Beattie Well Tank

Wenford Bridge Duty 637

Wadebridge Shed 1958

T9 30719

Nine Elms MPD

Capital Greyhound

LSWR T9 30730

Greyhound Stable

Three Bridges circa 1958

30936 Cranleigh

School's Days at the Brick

N Class 31833

Change for The Exe Valley Line

Dulverton

31847 N Class 2.6.0

The Withered Arm

Lydford

U1 Class Mogul 31905

Tonbridge Wells West circa 1960

Southern Workhorse

Billington 1913 Design K Class Mogul 32341

Brighton MPD

25th June 1957

Sunday spotter at Bricklayers Arms

Billington E6 No.32408

Down at the Brick

Bricklayers Arms

Marsh Rebuild C2X class 32538

Circa 1959

E4 Class 32563

Nine Elms Shed Pilot

Nine Elms Yard

Carrying the target for working on the Kent & East Sussex line Ex LB&SCR "Terrier", built in 1880 and formerly named Knowle stands outside the west end of St. Leonards shed.

Whilst the engine was based on the Isle of Wight in the 1930's as W14 Bembridge it was fitted with an extended bunker.

As BR 32678 after the closure of the K&ESR the engine was later moved to work on the Hayling Island Branch until withdrawal and sale to Butlins in 1964 and displayed at Minehead.

Bullied Q1 0.6.0

Nine Elms Goods

Nine Elms Shed

34023 Blackmore Vale

Wadebridge Main Line

LSWR in Cornwall

34057 Biggin Hill

Barnstaple Junction

6th June 1960

Bullied Air Smoothed Pacific

Battle of Britain at the Brick

34070 Manston on Bricklayers Arms Turntable

40454 Nottingham-Worcester-Swindon

East Midlander No.2

Wellingborough Jnc. (Midland & LNW)

40489 & 40454 RCTS East Midlander

A Pair of Deuces

Cheltenham Landsdown 6th May 1956

40504 Nottingham Midland

1st February 1955

Nottingham Blizzard

Glasgow to Kilmarnock Semie Fast   Last of the Summer Wine   Dumfries Station North West End

40686 Midland 2P 4.4.0 Hurlford Shed Kilmarnock Circa 1960

Hurlford Hero

Withdrawn 21 October 1961 from Hurlford.

Midland 2P 40686

Kilmarnock South Bay

Circa 1960

40686 Powers away from Kilmarnock

Volcanic Veteran

Circa 1960

Midland 2P 40687

Light Engine

Kilmarnock North End

Ex Midland Compound 40923

Perth Redundancy

Perth Motive Power Depot 29th June 1954

Midland Compound 40925 Pilots Jubilee

Midland Excellence

Derby London Road Jnc. 15th February 1958

41062 One of the last remaining Compounds

Last Rights

Derby Shed & Works Open day 30.08.58

Compound 41093

Northampton Line local

Rugby Arrival

Derby Compound 41173   _Old Glory_   Loughborough Water Troughs 16th August 1958

41277 Tutbury Jinnie

41313 Crossing the Taw River

Barnstaple Bridge

5th June 1960

42536 Stanier 3 Cylinder 2.6.4 Tank

Derby Works

Plaistow Pride

Loco spotters visit

Shed Bashing at Bury

Hughes Fowler Crab 42930

Buxton Minerals

Departs Buxton

42930 is banked out of Buxton

Buxton Signal Box

Buxton Minerals Banker

Boston allocated Ivatt Class 4 43066

Saxondale Express

Morning train from Skegness at Saxondale Notts

Ivatt Class 4　　　Melton Constable Running Shed　　　27th March 1955

Ivatt Flying Pig 43107

M&GNJR Main Line

Melton Constable

Ivatt Class 4

M&GN at Melton East

Melton Constable

76047 at Kirkby Stephen East

The Stainmore Railway

Circa 1960

43103 & 43013 Head Westbound Freight

1st September 1961

The Stainmore Line

Midland 4F 44342

Alsager Four at Winsford

Train of 16 ton mineral wagons

4F 0.6.0 with mixed freight

Setting out on Shap

Tebay

Fowler 4F 44576

Midland Four Derby Bound

Peckwash Mill Near Duffield

Roller Bearing fitted Caprotti Class 5

Elbows to the fore

Down Fast Kegworth

44817 Stanier Black Five

Derby Bound at Trent South Jnc.

Circa 1960

Stanier Class 5MT 44916

Mixed Freight Nottingham

Lenton South Junction

Stanier Black Five 44943

Taking the crossovers for Nottingham

Trent South Jnc

Double Headed Staniers Depart The Fort

Two Fives for Glasgow

Fort William 1959

Midland Up Main Line

The Thames Clyde Express

Kegworth Leicestershire

Stanier Black Five

Tebay Station

Southbound mixed freight.

45031 & Unknown Jubilee

London Express

Trent South Inc

Crewe North 45033 Pilots Unidentified Jubilee

The Bike Shed

Winsford Up Main

Home based Black Five 45035

Smoke and Grime

Warrington Dallam MPD 21st September 1952

Stanier Black Five 45043

Scout Green Shap

Scout Green Freight

Fowler 2.6.4 Tank assisting 45043

Scout Green Shap

Shap Banker

Stanier Black Five 45117

Northern Elegance

Inverness 14th May 1959

D5330 and three other BRCW Type 2 Diesels

Stanier Class Five 45117 Inverness May 1959

Changing Times

Crewe North Black Five 45240 & Jubilee

Northbound at Norton Bridge

Thompson Twin Set

45476 Pilots unknown Black Five

The Royal Highlander

Inverness 16th May 1959

Patriot 45537 Private E Sykes, VC

Whitmore Troughs

West Coast Main Line

The Stoke Up Line at Norton Bridge

Baby Scot on Stoke Line Express

45549 Un named Fowler Patriot

Stanier Jubilee

Norton Bridge

45555 Quebec

Jubilee Class 45557 New Brunswick

The Palatine

Midland Railway Trent South Junction

45651 Shovell

Loughborough Water Troughs

16th August 1958

45696 Arethusa

Carlisle Nymph

Loved by the River God

Jubilee 45728 & Black Fives

Defiance at Perth

Perth MPD

46126 Royal Army Service Corps

Skimming the Troughs

Whitmore Troughs 30th July 1960

Royal Scot 46153 The Royal Dragoon

The Comet

LNWR Staffordshire

46158 The Loyal Regiment

Kentish Town Scot at Stafford

Stafford Down Fast

Norton Bridge Staffordshire

Up Crewe line

46158 The Loyal Regiment

46203 Princess Margaret Rose

Royal Casualty

Failed at Carnforth

Stanier Class 8 Pacific

Princess Marie Louise

Winsford North of Crewe

46225 Duchess of Gloucester

Carlisle Right Away

Glasgow bound 31st May 1958

46225 Duchess of Gloucester   The Mid Day Scot   Carlisle 31st May 1958

46239 City of Chester

The Royal Scot

Down Fast at Stafford

46241 City of Edinburgh

A Tale of Two Cities

Glasgow Central

Stanier Pacific 46245

City of London

Norton Bridge

46248 City of Leeds

Scout Green Repeater

Scout Green Shap

Stanier Pacific 46253 City of St. Albans

Circa 1959

Norton Bridge Express

Ivatt Mogul 46496

Varsity Express

Cambridge

47979 on shed

Cricklewood Garratt

14A Cricklewood 13th March 1955

47981 Stands alongside the Garratt shed

The Old Order at Toton

18A Toton Notts 5th May 1956

48064 carrying an Overseal shed plate.

Going for a Burton

Light Engine South of Burton on Trent

Canklow allocated Class Eight 48515

Coates Park Consolidation

Lower Birchwood Collery Erewash valley

Ex LNWR 49281   Buxton 1959

Wheezer's Delight

Aspinall L&Y Pug 51241

Horwich Works Renewal

North British Built

Pickersgill on Parade

No 54472 Keith Loco

Pickersgill & Stanier Designs

Back to Back

63A Perth Motive Power 29th June 1954

Caly 0.4.4 tank 26th August 1953

68D Beattock Shed Yard

Beattock Banker

Pickersgill built McIntosh design 55237

Moffat Branch Train

Bay platform at Beattock

Caledonian 4.6.2 tank

Beattock shed yard 26th August 1953

Beattock Banker

1917 Built 4.6.2 Tank design.

Caledonian Pacific

Beattock Shed Banking Engine

Dugald Drummond 1883 design

Drummond Standard Goods

No 57361 at 66A Polmadie

1899 McIntosh Caledonian Jumbo 57620

Forres Shunter

Forres Morayshire

Midland 2F 58209

A Midland Gem

Derby Roundhouse

Gresley A4 Pacific 60030 Golden Fleece

Passing Newark South's Starter/Section signal

East Coast Elegance

A4 Pacific 60032 Gannet

East Coast Streamliner

Grantham

Gresley A3 Pacific 60042 Singapore

Top Shed

60050 Persimmon on G.N Diversion

G.N Summersaults

Sleaford 1st February 1959

60056 Centenary on Down Express

Sunset Express

Last Quarter Mile into Stoke Tunnel

Grantham

60066 Merry Hampton

Down Platform

York North end   Sunstar Sets Forth   2nd August 1958

60079 Bayardo

St Boswells

Waverley Magic

A3 Pacific 60093 Coronach

Gangers at Hawick

Approaches Hawick with Waverley Line Express

A3 Pacific 60096 Papyrus

Circa 1960

Haymarket Racehorse

60102 Sir Frederick Banbury   Grantham Lincolnshire

Great Northern Original

A1 Pacific 60131 Osprey   Grantham 1959

Northbound to Leeds

Gresley A3 60103 Flying Scotsman

Scotsman at The Old Vic

Nottingham Victoria 9th May 1953

A1 Pacific 60131 Osprey

Osprey flys North

Grantham Lincs.

Grantham

60132 Marmion

North End

South of Newark

60150 Willbrook

23rd May 1959

A2/2 Pacific 60505 rebuilt Gresley P2

Thane of Fife

Hitchin 5th September 1958

A2 Pacific 60528 Tudor Minstrel

Waverley Farewell

Hawick Station 23rd April 1966

Gresley V2 60836

Tweedmouth MPD

Standby Locomotive

Gresley V2 60873 Coldstreamer

Fifeshire Stopper

Inverkiething

Unidentified V2

Berwick on Tweed

The Royal Border Bridge

K2 61740 & B1 61168 22nd August 1959

Woodbine Crossing

Cleethorpe Road Crossing Grimsby Dock

B1 61180 Passing Dundee Loco Depot

Northern Departure

15th May 1959

Thompson B1 4.6.0

61327

31st March 1959

61327 Enters Goole Station

B1 61383 on The South Yorkshirsman

Heading for the Steel City

Sherwood Nottingham

Thompson Rebuild B16/3 61463

Lincoln Central

Lincoln Holiday Express

Rebuilt Holden B12 4.6.0 61530

Cambridge 23rd August 1959

Disposal Road

B17/6 61622 with GE Tender

Alnwick Castle

Yarmouth South Town 27th March 1955

Gresley B17/6 No. 61666 Nottingham Forest

Waiting Time

Cambridge 25th April 1959

Gresley B17 61672 West Ham United

Up The Hammers

Sratford Depot East London

Gresley K2 61763

Saxondale Notts

Ragtimer Seaside Special

Colwick K2 61773 at Saxondale

Heading Home

Skegness to Nottingham

Gresley K2 61784 with a train from Mallaig

West Highland Arrival

Fort William 8th June 1957

K2 61789 Loch Laidon & Coastal Steamer

Fort William Steamers

Fort William Old Station

Greasley K3 with GCR tender

Summer of 59

Saxondale Notts

D30 62436 Lord Glenvarloch

Scottish Lord in Residence

Hawick Loco Depot

Dunfermline based D30
62441 Black Duncan

Runs into
Inverkeithing

Past Waiting Haymarket

B1 61219

27th May 1958

158

D34 62477 on shed

Glen Dochart

Fort William 13th May 1959

D16 62568 Trent Jnc.

A Claud at Trent

8th February 1958

LNER D11 62667 Somme

Lincoln arrival at Nottingham Midland

East End 20th April 1957

Robinson D11/2 62668 Jutland   Lincoln Central

Lincoln Arrival

D49 Class 62733 Northumberland

Northern Territory

Perth Motive Power Depot   29th June 1954

The Old Order

Great Northern Splendour

GN J6 at Saxondale

J36 No.65300 Gets the fish wagons ready.

Shunting at The Fort

Fort William Goods

65300 Backs down onto its train.

Fort William Goods

Almost Ready to Go

J27 Believed to be 65874 at work with steel train.

Steel Country

Teesside North East England

1898 Vintage C12 Atlantic Tank

Shunts at Grantham 1953

Great Northern Survivor

Gresley V1 67617

Holmes J36 65233 Plumber

St Boswells a Waverley Byway

V3 Class 4 MT 2.6.2 Tank

Preparation at Helensburgh

28th June 1954

Thompson L1 2.6.4 Tank

All Stations to Grantham

Saxondale Notts

J88 68320 shares its berth with D49 Lanarkshire

St Margarets Shunter

64A Edinburgh St.Margarets Shed

Gresley N2 69581

Hatfield Stopper 1958

Hornsey Arrival

N7/3 69713 Doncaster Built

Beware of the Train Spotter

Stratford Running Shed London

Carrington Station

A5 Pacific Tank

Nottingham 1952

70007 Couer De Lion

Scourge of the Saracens

Cambridge

70021 Leaves Derby during the Works Open Day.

Morning Star

30th August 1958

70042 Lord Roberts

The Last Commander

Northbound at Norton Bridge

71000 Duke of Gloucester backs onto its train

Crewe 1961

The Final Chapter

Standard & Stanier Class 5's

Glasgow Express runs in at Fort William

Fort William

Eastfield Standard Five 73078

Arriving at Helensburgh

Road to the Isles

Nottingham based Standard Four 75063

Coates Park South

Lower Birchwood Collery Erewash Valley

Standard Class Four 80087

Bangor Tanks on Parade

Bangor Shed North Wales

Standard Four Tank 80111

Inverness Half Roundhouse

Conversation Piece

Ex Crosti Boilered 9F 92028

In The Works

Out with the Old and in with the New

Riddles 2.10.0 92105

Trent Junction

Circa 1959

Riddles Class 9F 92123

Trent Junction

Trackwork at Trent

9F 92163 With Conflats passes wooden posts & finials

Midland Signals

Approaches Trent Junction

92237 Heavey Freight

South Wales Minerals

Severn Tunnel Jnc.

Fort William to Glasgow

Tyndrum Horseshoe

In The Horseshoe

English Electric Type 4 D201

The New Order

Grantham 1958